# A DINOSAUR'S BOOK OF DINOSAURS

## KEITH BRUMPTON

ORCHARD BOOKS

This book is dedicated to my family, to
S. Bulman, and to dinosaurs everywhere

Text and illustrations © Keith Brumpton 1990
First published in Great Britain by
ORCHARD BOOKS
96 Leonard Street, London EC2A 4RH
Orchard Books Australia
14 Mars Road, Lane Cove NSW 2066
1 85213 236 1
A CIP catalogue record for this book
is available from the British Library
Printed in Belgium

# CALLING ALL DINOSAUR FANS....

At long last, here is a dinosaur book written *by* a dinosaur!

Not long ago, a large brown envelope dropped through my letter box. Inside, I found a copy of 'Roger Dinosaur's Book', a large exercise book full of pictures and notes made by a ten-year-old dinosaur called Roger.

I've no idea where it came from, because the postmark was smudged. And there wasn't a single word to say why Roger had chosen to send his package to me ... it's a mystery!

I thought Roger would like his book to be published, so here it is, exactly as he sent it ... a dinosaur's book of dinosaurs.

*Keith*

Keith Brumpton

## Author's ack~~nowlige~~ ~~acknowliing~~ thank you

There are so many dinosaurs who gave
me help with my book that I can't
remember them all. I would like to
thank Mum, Dad, and Lucy, and
Tricky Triceratops who lent me his pen.
Thank you also the football team, and
Bob the Brachiosaurus who didn't even
laugh when I missed that open goal last
~~weak~~ week.

Roger Dinosaur,
The Swamp
Sunset

p.s. Kenny our pet Pteranodon says can I
mention him as well!

# Contents

If you're wondering who this is, see page fourteen.

eyes -: brown
claws -: sharp
tail -: green.

full name: Roger Dinosaur

# Me when I was small..

(Some family photos taken when I was knee high to a dragon fly).

I was born at fern-time, and I weighed three rocks. Even then I seemed to like kicking my legs out. The Brontosaurus baby next to me was so long the photographer had to take three photos and stick them together!

← my first tooth. I used it to bite into a tasty tree.

⌐ Here I am eating my first leaves. As a baby I wasn't a big eater and could only manage a bush a day.

← my first steps. I climbed up mum's tail.

Dinachrome
SLIDE

Dinachrome
SLIDE

PROCESSED BY DINAK

↑ my first bath. I made quite a mess trying to kick the football under water!

9

# MEET MY FAMILY!

me ↗     Dad↓    Mum↓    Lucy↓

## MUM

On our family holiday last year we went walking in the hills.

Mum spends the day grazin She has done this e̶v̶ every da for the past thirty years. Mostly she's brilliant, like last birthday when she bought me notebook.

## LUCY

Lucy, my sister, is only six. She likes fooling around in the swamp and taking Kenny for his evening flap →

Camping! ↓

Dinachrome SLIDE

PROCESSED BY DINAK

Playing football with Lucy. Sometimes she plays for our t̶i̶k̶e̶ team.

Dinachrome SLIDE

PROCESSED BY DINAK

## Some good things about my family

1. Going away on holiday. Next year we're going to see the yummy-looking vegetation at Black River Volcano.

2. Lucy when she scores for our team at football.

3. When its someone's birthday and we go for a slap-up graze.

## Some bad things! ✗

1. Having to take Kenny for his flap when its cold outside.

2. Having to help Mum and Dad in the forest when everyone else is out playing football.

3. Lucy pulling my tail and then acting as if she hadn't.

4. Not being allowed out after sun-down because the Tyrannosaurus Gang are on the prowl.

# DAD

Dad often takes me for long walks. His favourite hobby is eating thick clumps of vegetation. He once ran the 800 metres in under a minute when being pursued by a Tyrannosaurus Rex!

# KENNY

is our pet Pteranodon. Every week Lucy takes him to obedience classes. He likes it when we throw him tree-trunks to fetch.

↖ Kenny having trouble with his swamp-shake. For more about Kenny see page 25.

# ...urhood ...

Meteorite shower
(ou need a
very strong
umbrella)

No, its not thunder,
just a herd of Brontosauruses
on the move

The airport is just nearby

THE FOREST. I'm not
allowed in here after dark
because of the Tyrannosaurus Gang.
Can you spot them?

They say its best to
start swimming when you're
young. Unless of course you're
a fish, in which case its best
to begin immediately !!!

Dermot and his friends playing football.
There's more about them on pages 22 + 23

This is my best friend,
**PARKY EUPARKERIA.**
He's the best player on our football team because he's such a fast runner.
He uses his tail to help him keep his balance.

ANOTHER GREASY TAKE-AWAY

← usually his food consists of flying insects, this is probably a treat.

Parky is ~~not~~ a great footballer, but sometimes he eats too much before the match!

If ever you are eating a tasty cockroach sandwich, don't let Parky see, or it will vanish before your eyes!

14

# MARCUS DIPLODOCUS

is the biggest dinosaur in our class.
When we go swimming he fills the whole pool, so we have to let him go in first. (It always takes him ages to get dried anyway!)

Sorry, Roger, can't stop!

One day Marcus decided to take up roller-skating, but it was a bit of a disaster... He lost control on a steep hill and Tricky and me had to help him out of the Swamp.

Because he is so big, Marcus has a huge appetite. When we made a birthday-cake for him it was so huge it took a hundred eggs. (If you like cooking, have a look at page 27).

There are some things about Marcus that even I still don't know. Maybe you could help me? ⟶

16

When he's trying to get to sleep does Marcus count Pteranodons instead of sheep?

Yes ☐

No ☐

Don't be silly ☐

How does Marcus Sleep at night?

☐ With his head between his legs?

☐ On his back?

☐ On his side?

Do you think Marcus lies in bed on sunday morning and reads the papers?

☐ Don't ask me

☐ Yes, if he has a week to spare

☐ Not if the Tyrannosaurus Gang are about!

Drat! The lads lost again.

If Marcus ever sneezed would he –

☐ Blow a hole in his handkerchief

☐ Flatten the nearest tree

☐ Put his hand over his mouth just in time

ATCHOOO!

P.S. for the answers to these questions, ask any passing Diplodocus. They're usually very friendly.

17

# TRICKY TRICERATOPS

is another of my friends. Tricky and his family like to go out to the plains and graze the grass there. He has a sharp beak which comes in very useful.

Uh-oh! If you want to know who is lurking here, turn to page 20

Tricky always asks if I know anyone who needs their lawn cutting. (It's a good way of earning pocket-money.)

Tricky has three horns on his bad head which are very useful for collecting litter.

\* Buy bone for Kenny.

BOOMF!

Tricky has the loudest knock at the front-door of anyone I know!

Watch out for **DANNY DEINONYCHUS!**

Danny comes from the other side of the swamp and he's quite a rough character. He has a very sharp claw on the end of his second toe, so it's a good idea not to argue with him.

sharp teeth

lots of muscles →

He copies Parky and uses his tail to balance while he runs.

← The terrible claw!!!

Its best to tip-toe past Danny without him seeing you.

A pair of nail-clippers would be a nice gift for Danny.

None of us other dinosaurs like playing football with Danny D, because he keeps bursting the ball with that terrible claw.

Not again!

Yet another foul!

19

FOOTBALL

VOLCANO VALLEY
team v
Amphibians
Saturday sunrise.
(or Lucy)
1. Dermot Stegosaur
2. Neville Cetiosaurus
3. Bob Brachiosaurus
4. Tricky Triceratops
5. Cuthbert Cetiosaurus
6. Brendan Plesiosaur
7. Parky *(captain).
8. Plateosaurus J.
9. Marcus Diplodocus.
10. Roger Dinosaur
11. Speedy.
meet by the swamp
tick if available.

← Our team is called Volcano Valley. Although I'm number ten I play in midfield. That's where the action is!

# A DANGEROUS PAGE...

(So please, not so much as a cough or a sneeze!)

This is probably the most dangerous page in the whole book. Which is why I'm hidden in the bushes with my skateboard, ready for a quick get-away...

This Tyrannosaurus is angry because Parky has just laughed at its little front legs. Some dinosaurs have no sense of humour!

the **TYRANNOSAURUS GANG** is best avoided!

They wander around eating almost any dinosaur in their path so you can guess why none of us go into the forest after dark!

Q. What is the most dangerous job in the world.
A. Being dentist to a Tyrannosaurus!

Keep that mouth wide open PLEASE!

It takes a lot of pulling to remove one bad tooth!

The entrance to the T. Gang's forest hideout.

If you ever come to this spot, start running QUICK!

# DERMOT STEGOSAURUS

Sits at the back of our class. He is very slow-moving and ~~very~~ often school is finished by the time he arrives!

When we had a sponsored run around the school-field, it took Dermot the whole summer holiday to do one lap.

SAVE ENERGY, STAY IN BED ALL DAY

Still we did raise fifty Dino-Pounds for our 'Plant-a-tree' campaign.

One of the Tyrannosaurus Gang thinks Dermot might make a tasty snack. He hasn't noticed the spikes on his tail yet!

Mostly Dermot uses the spikes on his tail to protect himself against attackers like the Tyrannosaurus Gang, but sometimes they come in handy for carrying the family shopping.

Of all my friends, **PROCCY PROCOMSOGNATHUS** is the most famous. He wins all the races in our valley and his main difficulty is getting his full-name onto his tracksuit —it's too long! Proccy is a good runner, but he's a bit of a big head. When he plays football for us, we have to pay him!

Well, I've been evolving hard for this one. I'll be surprised if I don't win...

( Lucy says I have to include this picture of Proccy being interviewed for our local paper.

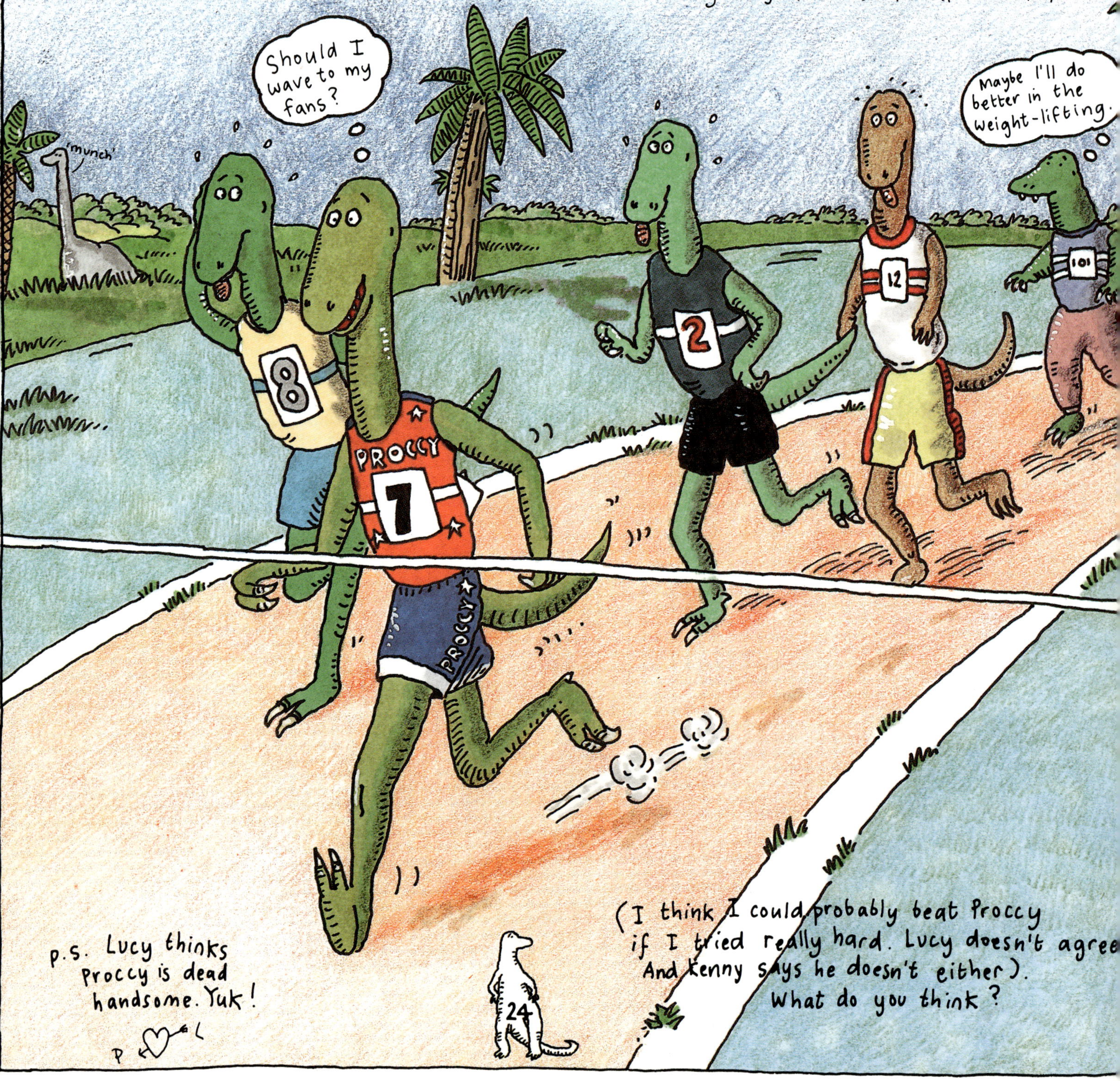

Should I wave to my fans?

'munch'

Maybe I'll do better in the weight-lifting.

p.s. Lucy thinks Proccy is dead handsome. Yuk!

P♡L

24

( I think I could probably beat Proccy if I tried really hard. Lucy doesn't agree. And Kenny says he doesn't either).
What do you think?

# KENNY PTERANODON

is our pet. Though he is only little at the moment, Mum says when he's fully grown he'll have to sleep outside. And we'll need a really strong bird-table! Kenny's favourite food is fish, but as a treat we sometimes give him jellyfish and ice cream. Because he needs a lot of exercise we take it in turns to take him out. Lucy takes him out most.

Unfortunately, because his muscles are so weak, kenny isn't a great flier. In fact he never goes much further than the back garden.

It's nice to get off the leash now and then

↑ Kenny flying overhead

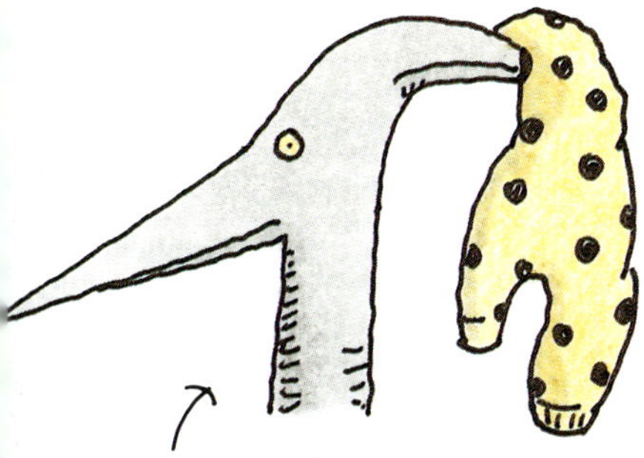

↑ Kenny has a big crest on the back of his head. He uses this to hang his pyjamas on.

A poem about Kenny

His body is bald
Without a single feather
So he doesn't like flying
When it's rainy weather.

His action isn't smooth
You can hear him flap and creak
As he tries to catch a fish or two
Using his pointy beak.

Roger D.

# ROGER'S RECIPE PAGE

Kenny's fish pie
Swoop down to the river and scoop up a fish in your beak. Cook over hot volcano lava for five minutes then gobble up.

(serves one).

Bob's health tip
Bob Brachiosaurus recommends eating more fresh fruit and leaves from the tops of the trees.

If you want to get the best young shoots you'll have to get up early!

Roger's elevenses
Take eleven pieces of tree bark, dip them in the sea to add flavour, and eat quickly before Parky sees them.

Yum!

There's nothing nicer than an open-air picnic!

It's very important to try out the ingredients first!

A joke!

Q. How d'you make a milk-shake?
A. Balance it on the ground when a herd of Brachiosauruses are walking by.

watch out for insects like this ... They're big enough to carry off your nosh!

27

# GETTING IN SHAPE DINOSAUR - STYLE...

Start by trying to touch your tail ten times. It's not as easy as it looks!

The Brontosaurus family out for a fun-run.

Before training its very important to warm-up first. Proccy recommends standing next to a volcano.

giant fossils

Parky →

Its always a good idea to get a keen friend to come along and train with you. Looks like Parky has been having too many flying-insect suppers!

Being chased by a Tyrannosaurus is very good exercise, but its a bit dangerous!

Tricky doesn't do much sport, but he likes a game of coytes now and then.

28

# R♡MANTIC DIN♡SAURS

(a useful section if you ever fall in love with a dinosaur)

smack!

...or the wrong shape

Dinosaurs don't kiss very often, partly because we're either too ugly ...

... or just too tall !

Instead we link tails !

This is Lynsey Corythosaurus, the dinosaur next door. She is carrying a piece of fern I gave her. Unfortunately her parents are moving to a new swamp down south, so I don't suppose I shall see her again. Drat !

Tricky gets the most Valentine's cards, but only because they blow onto his horns.

Some dinosaurs have no style !

Fancy going out for a bite to eat, darling?

A lot of dinosaurs change the colour of their skin when they're out on a date. I usually turn pink !

Five gifts any dinosaur would like —

1. A piece of fern or fresh shoot.
2. A bottle of fresh swamp-water.
3. A Rochdale United football scarf.
4. My address and telephone number (only joking!)
5. A nice book — something by the Brontosaurus Sisters for example.

# COULD YOU BE A DI

In the Dino-Scouts we have to learn all about tracks and trails and how to survive in the wild. You can try some of the tests. The answers are on page 32.

1 Imagine you go out at night. How many of these dinosaurs could you recognise?

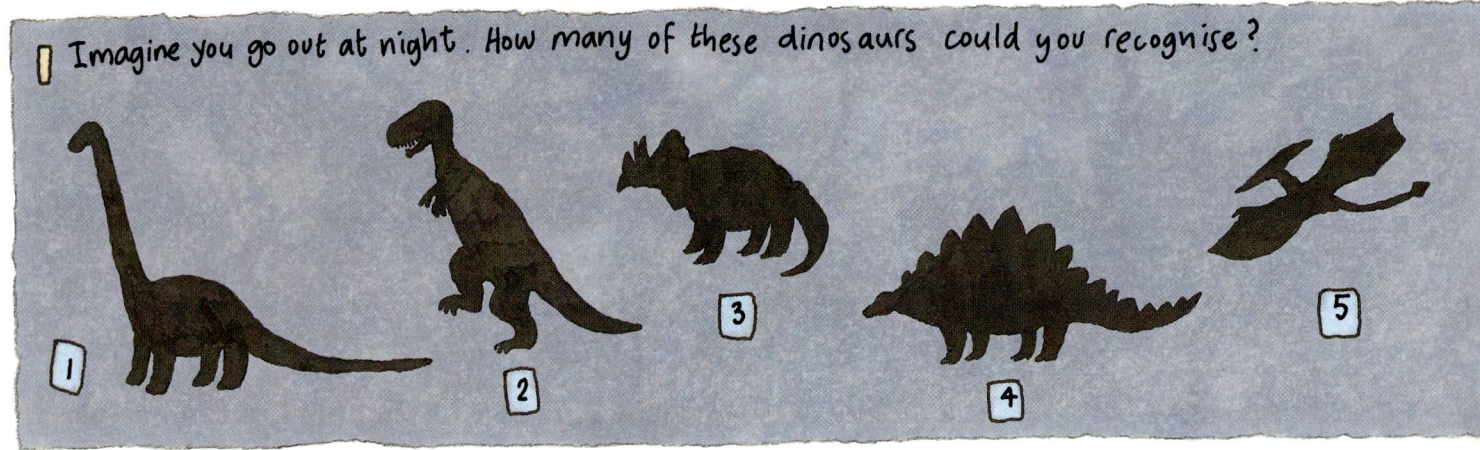

1
2
3
4
5


## 2. DINOSAUR TRACKS

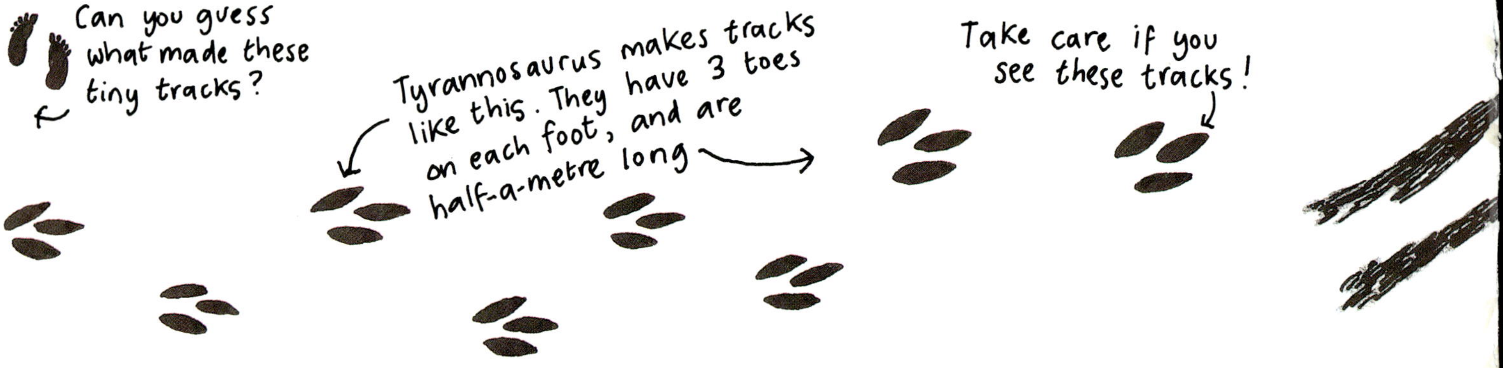

Can you guess what made these tiny tracks?
Tyrannosaurus makes tracks like this. They have 3 toes on each foot, and are half-a-metre long
Take care if you see these tracks!


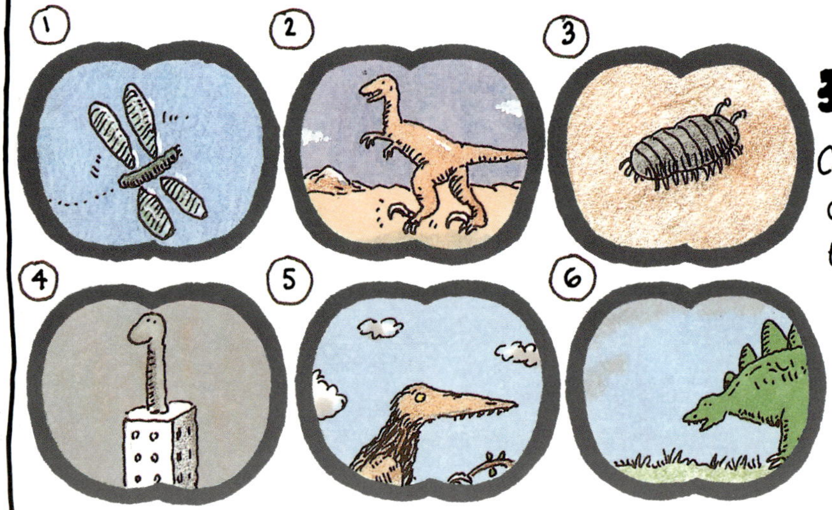

1
2
3
4
5
6


## 3. OBSERVATION

Can you guess what creatures I can see through my binoculars?

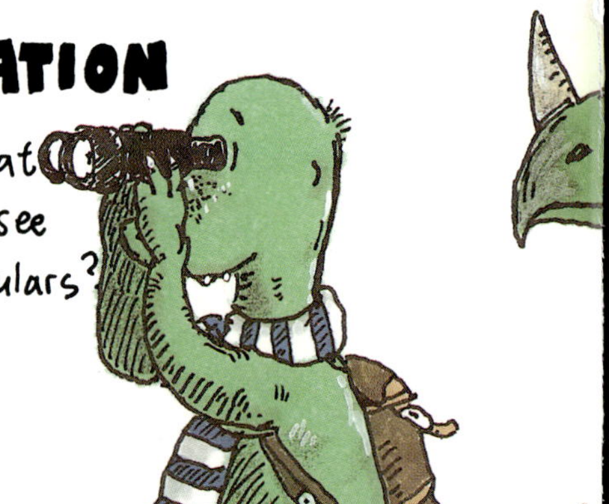

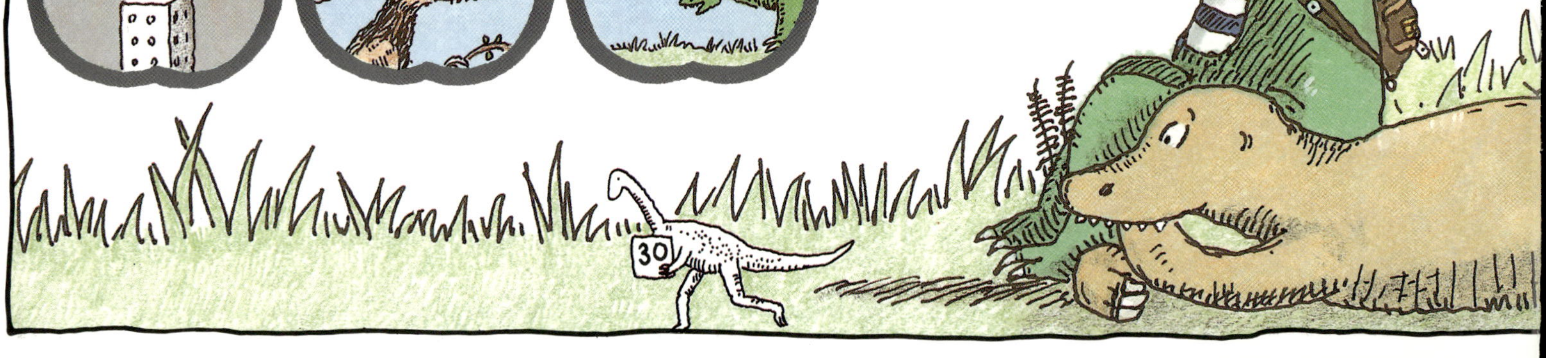

# O-SCOUT LIKE ME?

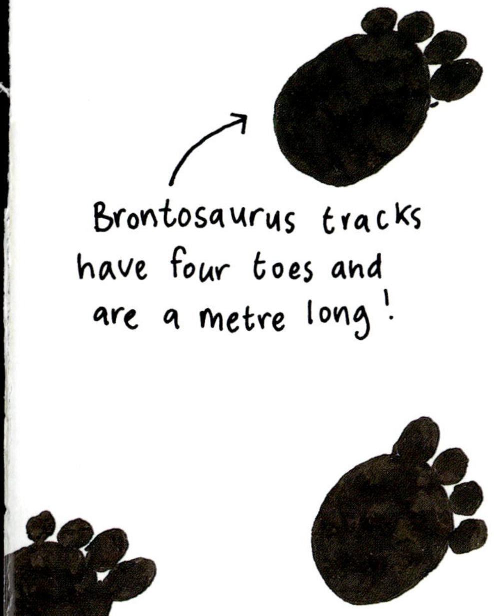

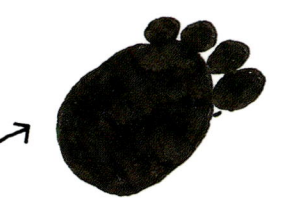

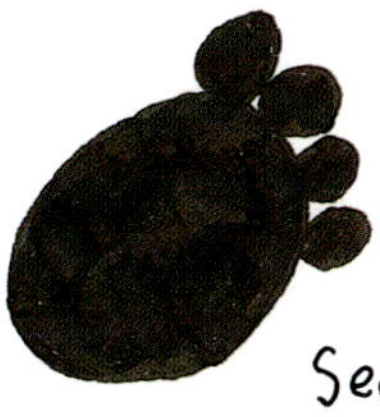

Brontosaurus tracks have four toes and are a metre long!

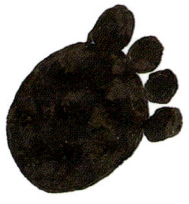

there is also a mark where their tail trails along the ground

## 4. ROGER'S AMAZING MAZE

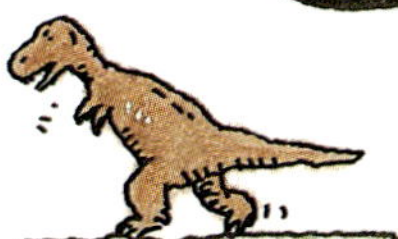

See if you can escape the Tyrannosaurus Gang and make your way safely to Tricky's home...

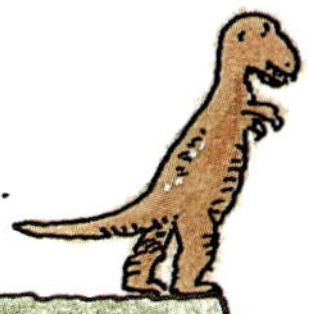

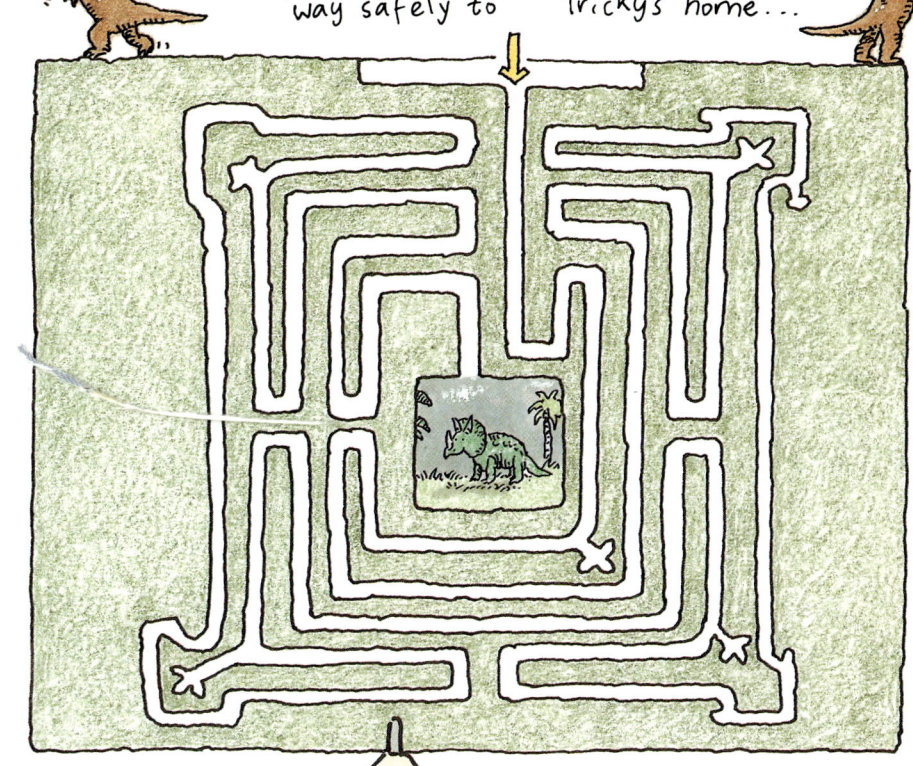

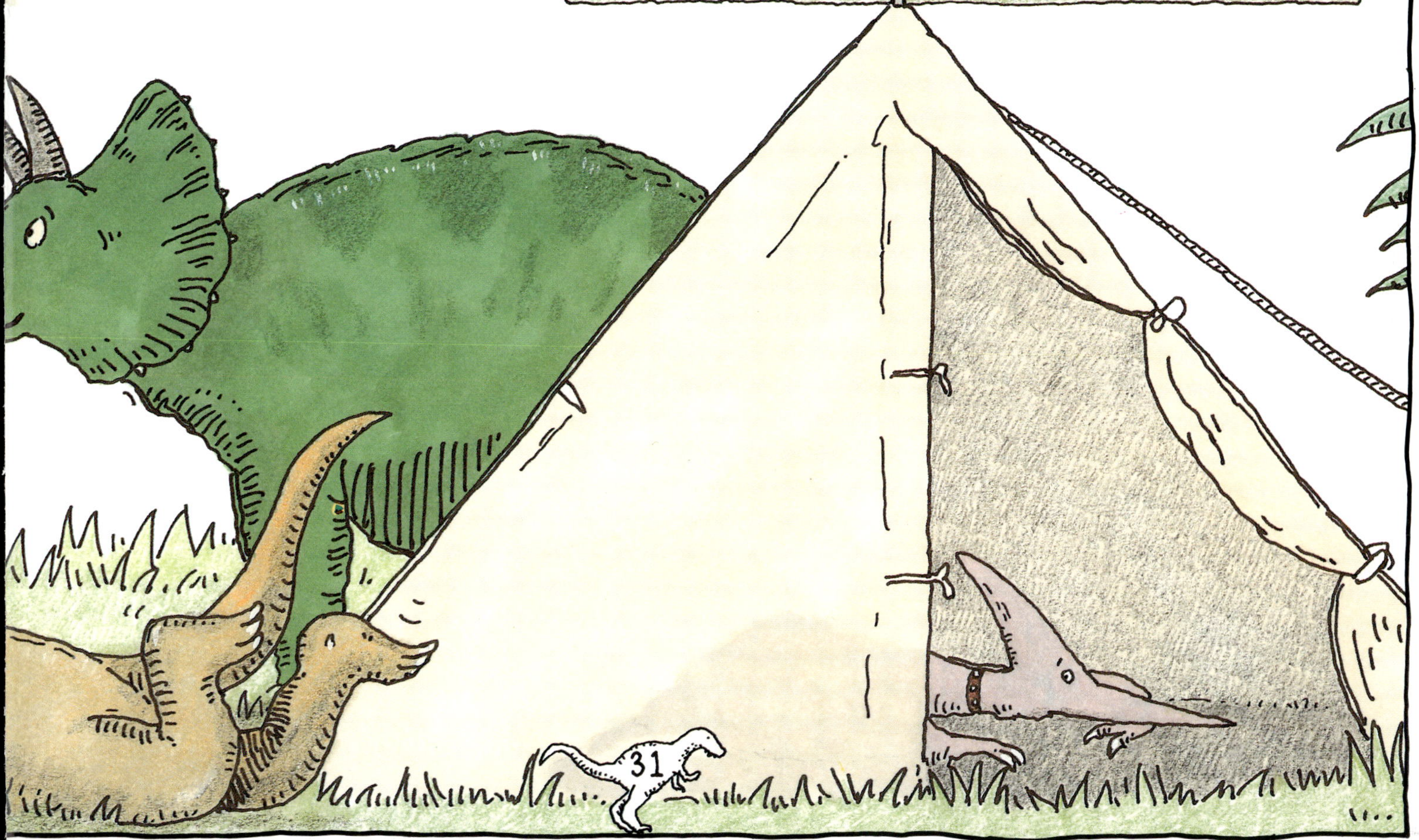

☆ Here are the answers to my **Dino-scout** quiz... ☆

one
1. Marcus Diplodocus
2. One of the Tyrannosaurus Gang
3. Tricky Triceratops
4. Dermot Stegosaurus
5. Kenny Pteranodon

two    A human being made the tiny tracks!

three
1. A Dragon fly
2. A Brontosaurus
3. Danny Deinonychus
4. Rhamphy Rhamphorynchus
5. A giant millipede
6. Dermot Stegosaurus

Dino-

← our badge

scout

How did you do? If you got more than five right you would probably make a very good Dino-Scout!

— Roger D.

And that's the end of Roger's book. I hope you enjoyed it. One day I hope he will get in touch with me again ... Maybe he'll write another book! If he does, I promise to let you know.

Keith Brumpton